Advent

DEVOTIONALS & LITURGIES

Written by pastors and members of Coram Deo Church

Copyright © 2023 Coram Deo Church. Scripture quotations are from the ESV® Bible (The Holy Bible, English Standard Version®), copyright © 2001 by Crossway, a publishing ministry of Good News Publishers. Used by permission. All rights reserved.

TABLE OF CONTENTS

FOREWORD 5

THANKSGIVING DAY

A Prayer for Thanksgiving Day (Brynn James) 7

WEEK 1

Christmas Family Ties (Pastor Jon Needham) 11

The Promised Son of Christmas (Pastor Derrek Busha) 15

WEEK 2

The Glory of the Virgin Birth (Pastor Jon Needham) 19

The Promised Lamb of Christmas (Pastor Kim Highfield) .. 23

WEEK 3

Herod, the Grinch (Pastor Jon Needham) 27

The Promised King of Christmas (Pastor Brandon Johnston) . 31

WEEK 4

Christmas According to Moses (Pastor Rusten Harris) 35

The Promised City of Christmas (Pastor Ryan James) 39

CHRISTMAS DAY

A Prayer for Christmas Morning (Brynn James) 45

Foreword

Merry Christmas, and welcome to Coram Deo's Advent Devotional and Liturgy guide! Advent is a unique season for reflecting on and celebrating the birth of our Lord and Savior, Jesus Christ. In addition to all your beloved and perhaps quirky traditions, we hope this simple guide will draw you to the awe and glory of the virgin-born, manger-veiled Messiah. Here is how it works.

Each Sunday of Advent at Coram Deo Church, we will examine the Christmas story as told in Matthew's Gospel. Each Sunday sermon text will have a supplemental Lord's Day devotional. I suggest reading these on Sunday evenings.

Additionally, we have written four midweek devotionals examining how the birth of Christ fulfills God's promises in the Old Testament. Liturgies for prayer and reflection accompany all eight devotionals. You will also find special liturgies for Thanksgiving Day and Christmas morning to help you enter those special days with gratitude, perspective, and worship. All devotionals and liturgies are great for family, group, or personal readings.

Lastly, the climax of Advent is our Christmas Eve Candlelight services. They are both simple and beautiful, consisting of traditional Christmas carols, a short homily, and of course, lighting candles. Christmas Eve Candlelight service times are 2, 3, 4, and 5 p.m. We will also gather for regular Sunday worship on the morning of Christmas Eve at 8, 9:30 and 11 a.m.

I pray that God will bless you this Advent season with renewed hope, love, joy, and peace.

Merry Christmas!

Jon Needham
Lead Pastor
Coram Deo Church

A Prayer for Thanksgiving Day

By Brynn James

> *¹ Oh come, let us sing to the LORD;*
> > *let us make a joyful noise to the rock of our salvation!*
> *² Let us come into his presence with thanksgiving;*
> > *let us make a joyful noise to him with songs of praise!*
> *³ For the LORD is a great God,*
> > *and a great King above all gods.* — Psalm 95:1–3 (ESV)

Gracious Father, King above all gods.
Your children gather to worship and rejoice
in the abundant provision of your hand!
O Lord, all we need thy hand has provided.
We give thanks for the creation of all that is fair.

We worship today not with pews and pulpits,
but with cutlery and good cheer.

Thanksgiving Day

Before us, a buffet full of delight for the eye, stomach,
and soul. May our feast tell the story of your goodness!
We are people of the table,
and the joy of the Lord is our strength.

Earnestly, we seek the almighty giving and forgiving God.
We confess that we often forget how lavishly
our sins have been absolved.
Not only has our wickedness been washed away,
but we've been summoned to the feast.
You have given us a seat at the banquet table where
Christ is the host and the meal alike.
May this Thanksgiving Day remind us that we,
the unlovely, have been welcomed
into the presence of the King.
And into your presence, we march!
We come with jolly gratitude, fork in hand.
Make merry this home, O Lord. Bless this table and
everything that will happen around it in the season ahead.

Though the way is dark and the road narrow, may this
household shine brightly as a waypost of comfort and
joy, beckoning weary pilgrims on their way to Zion's city.
Let this meal be but a luminary in the constellation of the
Christian walk, showing us the way home.
In the face of lies, danger, and death,
we raise our glasses and our voices.
Let our feasting, like our joy, be our testimony.

A Prayer for Thanksgiving Day

That we might declare, at a table in the presence of
our enemies, that you alone satisfy the desire
of every living thing.

May the sounds that punctuate our meal
ring out in glad celebration:
Glasses clinking.
Rowdy laughter.
Fork scraping plate.
The panting of a hopeful dog under the table.
Each one proclaims, "No King but Christ."
Our joyful noise unto the Lord.
Bless our labors as we prepare, enjoy, and tidy up
after this meal.
Accept our humble hospitality and grant the increase.
Multiply our joy and gratitude, O Great God, giving
us eyes to see the gifts we take for granted and a new
awareness of our Father's hand, making all things new.
Let this meal inaugurate our season of longing as
we look forward to Christmas and even further
to the wedding feast of the lamb.
By heavenly help, may we live out this joy, rehearsing for
the day when we will taste everlasting glory.

Amen.

WEEK 1 — Lord's Day Evening

Christmas Family Ties

Devotional and Liturgy by Pastor Jon Needham

> *¹ The book of the genealogy of Jesus Christ, the son of David, the son of Abraham.* — Matthew 1:1 (ESV)

Christmas is fast approaching. It's not just a time of looking forward to what lies ahead. It's also a time to reflect on that past. Chances are, at some point, you will find yourself gathered with friends and family, eating cookies, and telling stories. Perhaps an old photo that has been hibernating for years will surface, awakening long-forgotten memories of past generations. It is in the context of our past generations that we most fully understand who we are.

Similarly, if we want to understand who Christ, the child of Christmas, is fully, we must first understand the generations that came before him. Matthew carefully records the genealogy of Christ for us, tracing it back some forty-two generations. Among the ordinary people listed, two names stand out as being uniquely significant: Abraham and David. Both Abraham and David played important roles in redemptive history. But what is perhaps most important about these men is not who they were but what God had promised them.

To Abraham, an old man with a barren wife, God promised a gigantic family through whom the entire earth would be blessed. Somehow, the chaos and curse of sin, which had infected all of creation, would be overturned through Abraham's future descendant, who is Christ (Galatians 3:16).

To David, the King of Israel, God promised an everlasting throne (2 Samuel 7:12 & 16). Though David's reign would come to a tragic end and his own house would be divided, at some point in the distant future, God would re-establish David's throne in righteousness.

Forever.

Generations would come and generations would go, waiting to see how God would keep his Word. Though the faithfulness of God's people would wax and wane, the promises God made to Abraham and David would stand secure.

As Matthew tells the story of Christ's birth, he first reminds us of the past. He shows us that God is faithful. What God has promised, God has done. As we enter into this Advent season, may we be reminded that God always keeps his Word. When the path appears dark, when the way is unknown, when God's hand is unseen, and when his presence is unfelt, remember that he always keeps his promises.

Always.

Liturgy

Ever faithful God,
You give your Word, and you keep your Word.

Your promises to Eve, Abraham, and David,
all of them kept in your perfect timing.

As generations come and generations go,
waiting, wondering, questioning…
You remain faithful, never wavering
from all you have promised.

What you speak, you deliver.
Against all odds, your truth stands forever.

An old man, a barren wife, a divided family…

Week 1: Lord's Day Evening

Nothing can thwart your plan.

Nothing.

God of promises, teach us to trust in you.
When all else fails, may we stand upon your Word.

Teach us to trust your timing, your plan, your wisdom, and your power.
Teach us, O God, to question our skepticism.

When doubt creeps in, bring us back to the manger where we find your promised Word, given to us.

Remind us once again, O LORD, that you are faithful.

Amen.

WEEK 1 — Midweek Evening

The Promised Son of Christmas

Devotional by Pastor Derrek Busha, Liturgy by Pastor Aaron Kuhns

> *¹⁵ I will put enmity between you and the woman, and between your offspring and her offspring; he shall bruise your head, and you shall bruise his heel."* — Genesis 3:15 (ESV)

Advent is the season we revisit every year to remember and celebrate that Christ has arrived and given us new life and salvation. But often, we don't consider the long unfolding story and drama that precedes his birth. The story leading up to the birth of Christ is full of sin, rebellion, pain, and strife. It's a story of mankind trying, and often failing, to hang on to what God had promised at the beginning in Genesis 3.

Sin entered the world through Adam and Eve. God

promised Eve a child, a son, who would crush the serpent, put an end to sin, and undo the curse. Eve mistakenly thought her first child, Cain, would be the promised savior. Genesis 4:1 records her joy: "I have gotten a man with the help of the Lord." But, he would grow up only to dishonor her and dishonor God by killing his younger brother.

Cain's sin and rebellion would set the tone for the subsequent generations of God's people, Israel. They would tear their way through history looking for fulfillment and satisfaction not in God, but on their own terms and conditions. Nothing but difficulty and trouble came because of their sin, aided and enticed by the devil himself.

Similarly, our lives are often filled with desires to find hope and fulfillment in other things: careers, marriages, children, homes, etc.—things that are good but incapable of giving us complete satisfaction.

Christmas interrupts everything and serves as a much-needed reminder that the hope and salvation we long for can be found, but not in the usual places.

The promised child arrives in the humble beginnings of the manger scene. Jesus stops the seemingly endless cycle of sin and provides the hope that the world has been clamoring for. Jesus, Israel's true son, does not come to kill his brother. Instead, he arrives to be killed ***for*** his brother, providing the true gift of Christmas that we all need.

Mary's son Jesus was born at the right time, bringing an end to the sin that started with the first family. Jesus is the son that Eve was promised, the King that Israel was waiting for, the Savior that mankind needs.

God kept his promise. He gave his only Son. The whole world is invited to peek into the manger to see and proclaim that the promised Savior has arrived!

Liturgy

Ancient of Days,
You know our history better than we know ourselves.
You have witnessed the rise and fall of nations
and so-called saviors.
You see our own affections bounce between gadgets and people and trends.
Though we grasp at straw and vapor for satisfaction,
forgetting your goodness, you still draw near to us.
Your love still abounds.
O Redeemer, break the cycle of our sin.
We were brought out of our own Egypt,
yet we keep looking back.
Turn our eyes from worthless things.
Help us remember how you rescued us

Week 1: Midweek Evening

from death on the cross
And secured our adoption into your family.
O Spirit of God, open our eyes.
Outshine the fading promises of this world.
Show us your glory through the beauty of Scripture.
Let the Gospels awaken our hearts anew with amazement.
Your love is unmatched.
Your grace is overwhelming.
Your power is transforming.
Your wisdom is surprising.
Your faithfulness is unending.
Amen.

WEEK 2 — Lord's Day Evening

The Glory of the Virgin Birth

Devotional and Liturgy by Pastor Jon Needham

> *²³ "Behold, the virgin shall conceive and bear a son, and they shall call his name Immanuel" (which means, God with us).*
> — Matthew 1:23 (ESV)

More than any other season, Christmas is full of wild tales and unbelievable stories. Flying reindeer, animated snowmen with corn cob pipes, an angry green monster who lives in a dump, and a hidden magical city located up north are just a few examples. We love these silly tales. They make us laugh and give us joy. But nobody expects us to take those stories seriously.

The real Christmas story is not like that. It simultaneously claims something incredible and expects us to believe it. At the very center of the Christmas story is the unapologetic claim that Mary, the mother of Jesus, was a virgin and that her child was conceived of the Holy Spirit (Matthew 1:20). To emphasize the prophetic, miraculous, and historical nature of this event, Matthew reminds us that this was foretold by Isaiah, the prophet, some seven centuries before Jesus' birth.

If we're honest, the virgin birth claim sounds ridiculous, perhaps even unbelievable. Maybe people way back then were more susceptible to those kinds of stories, but we live in the scientific age, and we all know that a virgin birth is impossible in our world. And therein lies the problem.

We do not live in our world. We live in God's world. This is not **our** story. This is **God's** story. He created everything out of nothing. He created humanity from the dust; Eve from Adam's side. He is the God who parted the Red Sea; the God who caused bread to rain from heaven and water to flow from a rock. He is the God of Christmas—the God of virgin birth.

Don't let the virgin birth be a stumbling block for you. Instead, let it be the door to understanding that God is God and that he is able to do anything he wants. May God remind us again and again this Christmas season, that nothing is too difficult for him.

Nothing.

Liturgy

Almighty Triune Creator God,

Out of nothing, you brought forth the world.
Out of darkness, light.
You said, "Let there be" and there was.
And it was very good.

Ages ago, you promised a virgin-born king.
A sign for those patiently waiting.
A light for those walking in darkness.

To the virgin Mary, you announced a child,
conceived by the power of the brooding Spirit.

Out of the virgin's womb, you brought forth our Savior,
that by him, we might be brought forth out of slavery.

At the manger, O Lord, you took upon yourself our flesh,
trading heaven for earth,
angels for shepherds,
the throne for a manger.

That on the cross, you might take upon yourself our sin.
Trading your righteousness for our wretchedness.

That from the grave you might rise, so we too might
become sons of the living God.

Week 2: Lord's Day Evening

A gift too costly.
A work too marvelous.
And yet, you have done it.

Eternal Incarnate Word,
We praise you in endless awe and wonder.

Amen.

WEEK 2 — Midweek Evening

The Promised Lamb of Christmas

Devotional by Pastor Kim Highfield, Liturgy by Pastor Aaron Kuhns

> [8] *Abraham said, "God will provide for himself the lamb for a burnt offering, my son." So they went both of them together.*
> — Genesis 22:8 (ESV)

Christmas is the best. As it approaches, each day is filled with new experiences and old memories intertwined. While we give and receive gifts on other occasions, the excitement and joy of Christmas gifts surpasses all others. It's because Christmas is undergirded by the fact that we are celebrating the greatest gift ever given: the promised lamb of Christmas—Jesus.

The Old Testament is full of hints and shadows of the

Week 2: Midweek Evening

promised Christmas lamb, but the story of Abraham and Isaac tops them all. Abraham's faith wasn't a theoretical faith; his was a practical faith developed from walking with God and witnessing his faithfulness firsthand, including the miraculous birth of his beloved son Isaac. But God commanded Abraham to offer Isaac as a burnt offering. In the Old Testament, burnt offerings served as a temporary propitiation for sin. They also symbolized total commitment and surrender to God. However, these offerings were inadequate and could not deal with the problem of sin. Consequently, they needed to be repeated regularly.

This created a problem as Abraham only had one true promised son. He had no other sacrifice to make, no other offering to give. Jesus said, "Whoever loves father or mother more than me is not worthy of me, and whoever loves son or daughter more than me is not worthy of me" (Matthew 10:37). This was God's test for Abraham. Was Abraham willing to give his only son, the son of promise, back to God? Would Abraham trust in God's provision? Abraham passed God's test and received the substitutionary gift that God provided through the ram stuck in the thicket.

When John the Baptist saw Jesus, he said, "Behold, the Lamb of God, who takes away the sin of the world" (John 1:29). Those words should have clicked for the Jews and they should click for us. The gift God gave Abraham was a shadow of the gift he has given us in Jesus. He is not only the fulfillment of God's promises to Abraham; he is the lamb of God, born in a manger, and sacrificed on the cross for us. Because of him, our sins are forgiven. He is the King who blesses the nations and rules forever. He is the promised lamb of Christmas.

Liturgy

Almighty Father,
Your wisdom is great and our understanding is so small.
Your love is not divided, misguided, or tainted like our love.
There is no one more trustworthy than you,
yet we confess that obedience is often difficult.
We struggle to believe that your ways are best,
that your law is good.
Yet you have proven over and over that
you are the perfect Father, the greater Abraham.
You are worthy of our obedience, God of all creation.
Your heart for the broken, ashamed, and lost
pours out of the pages of Scripture.
We could not save ourselves, so you sent your Son.
We could not revive our dead hearts,
so you sent your Spirit.

Week 2: Midweek Evening

Teach us to trust you,
even in the valley of the shadow of death.
For you are with us.

Amen.

WEEK 3 — Lord's Day Evening

Herod, the Grinch

Devotional and Liturgy by Pastor Jon Needham

> ³ *When Herod the king heard this, he was troubled, and all Jerusalem with him;* — Matthew 2:3 (ESV)

There are a number of words that we typically associate with Christmas and Advent. Joy, peace, hope, love, gifts, trees, carols, lights, Red Ryder BB guns…you could probably go on and on. But I'm guessing none of us would ever associate the word "troubled" with Christmas. After all, what could be so troubling about an overlooked infant placed in a manger, born into a nobody family in a nowhere town?

As it turns out, quite a bit.

Week 3: Lord's Day Evening

Matthew tells us that visiting Magi from the East, (frequently referred to as wise men), being led by a divinely directed star, came seeking the newborn king of the Jews so that they might worship him. They inquired of Herod where they might find this infant king. This is what troubles Herod, ultimately igniting his infanticidal rage. Herod's problem was not that he didn't understand who Jesus was. Rather, he knew exactly who this child was… and he hated him.

Herod knew that Jesus was the prophesied and long-awaited true King of Israel. Herod was just a fraud. Jesus' birth meant that Herod's knee must bow and that his tongue confess that Christ is Lord (Philippians 2:10-11). Corrupt King Herod was willing to make any compromise that was politically expedient to his continued faux reign. But the one thing he could not do is acknowledge this newborn child as the rightful true King…his King. For Herod, the birth of Christ was a threat; an unwelcome heavenly invasion.

As we approach this Christmas, may we not be blinded or intoxicated by mere sentimentality. Yes, we ought to enjoy this wonderful season with all its festivities, wonder, and traditions. But we must remember that the birth we are remembering and celebrating is the birth of the King. If we seek to protect and maintain our own autonomous rule and reign, we too like Herod will find this time quite troubling. But, if, like the Magi and the shepherds, we approach the manger to worship with humility and awe, we will find our hearts filled with joy, our sins forgiven, and our lives rightly ordered under the gracious rule of the Christmas King.

Liturgy

Almighty King,
Lord, God, and ruler of all.

All things were created by you.
All things are sustained by you.
All things exist for you.
We are no exception.

In sadness, we confess that like Herod, at times,
we see your birth and your rule as a threat.

We think we know better, that autonomy is the way to freedom, that submission to you means slavery.

We are wrong.

Lord, forgive us.

Like the Magi, lead us to yourself.

Week 3: Lord's Day Evening

Remind us that it is only in submission to you
that we can ever truly be free.
Our freedom is why you were born.
Our joy was purchased through your anguish,
our life through your death.

In joy, we gladly confess there is no greater name, and no higher throne, no greater dominion than yours.

Teach our knees to cheerfully bow.

Teach our tongues to gladly confess that
you and you alone are Lord.

Teach us O Lord, to delight in your sovereign rule
over all of creation.

Amen.

WEEK 3 — Midweek Evening

The Promised King of Christmas

Devotional by Pastor Brandon Johnston, Liturgy by Pastor Aaron Kuhns

> *[16] And your house and your kingdom shall be made sure forever before me. Your throne shall be established forever.'"*
> — 2 Samuel 7:16 (ESV)

One of my favorite Christmas traditions is to drive around at night and look at Christmas lights. This often includes cookies being passed around the van as I awkwardly sing Christmas carols at the top of my lungs. There are some verses where I can't help but belt out the lyrics. "Hark! The Herald Angels Sing" is one of those carols. There is something about singing "Glory to the newborn King!" that causes me to sing more vigorously. The Christmas story is full of kings and the promise that God would send his people a special king. God made a promise to King David that one day, he would raise up a new kind of king. A better king. An eternal king.

King David experienced God's faithfulness all throughout his life. From God's deliverance from danger when he was a shepherd to God's deliverance when enemies surrounded him, God always showed himself to be faithful and true. But what about God's kingdom after David draws his last breath? What would become of his family and his people? As a newer father, I've thought, "How will my family be when my time comes? Will they be cared for? Will they be protected? Will they be provided for?" I would imagine this burden may be even greater for David as he considers all of God's people.

The good news of Christmas is that God has kept his promise to David. God promised he would raise up an heir to the throne from David's own family. It was not simply that God would raise up another king. God would establish a king like no other. He promised a kingdom that would last forever and a King who would reign forever. Through this Everlasting King, God would conquer sin, ensuring God's people were never enslaved to it again. God's King would be victorious over death. No longer would the grave have the last word, but God's King, the living Word, would speak the words of eternal life.

The good news of Christmas is that this promised King has come and his name is Jesus. He is God's King who conquered the enemies of sin and death for his people. He now sits on the eternal throne that God prepared for him. He rules over his enemies, and his people are blessed.

To the one true King! Cheers!

Liturgy

O Ruler of all,
In the midst of uncertainty, you remain stable.
Through overwhelming changes, you remain constant.
You cannot be simplified into a God who only loves
or only judges.
Your mercy and longsuffering flow through
the Old Testament.
Your holiness and justice are not diminished in the New.
You truly are the same yesterday, today, and tomorrow.
How we long for an anchor in the midst of our storm!
But our King is not far off.
The Almighty entered history as a helpless baby.
The Holy One reached out to
the unclean and contagious outcasts.
The Righteous One sat down

Week 3: Midweek Evening

with sinners and tax-collectors.
Our Savior gave himself up to be beaten,
mocked and executed
This King was rejected, not because he had changed,
but because the world did not know who he had always been.
O Lord, give us eyes to see your unchanging character.
May our hearts pour forth thankfulness
at the honor of knowing you.
Help us walk with our King daily
and to be wise in each season.

Amen.

WEEK 4 — Lord's Day Evening

Christmas According to Moses

Devotional and Liturgy by Pastor Rusten Harris

> *[15] This was to fulfill what the Lord had spoken by the prophet, "Out of Egypt I called my son."* — Matthew 2:15 (ESV)

"It's the most wonderful time of the year!" Yes, indeed! My heart agrees with a warm and cheerful "Amen!" I love Christmastime: the feasting, the presents, the family gatherings, the decorations, and the lights! Christmas is a wonderful and joyous time.

But this time of celebration came into our world the way that light invades a dark morning. When Christ was born, he was not born into friendly territory, but rather behind enemy lines. Even before Jesus was born, he was the target of an assassination by the tyrant King Herod. He was born into conflict with real evil because he was born to be our deliverer.

Matthew says Christ's coming fulfilled the word of the prophets. If you listen closely, you can hear echoes of God's great deliverances: A dreaming Joseph. A cruel king who massacres children. Egypt. Escape. But it's clear something greater than the Exodus is here.

We read of the fulfillment of Hosea 11:1: "When Israel was a child, I loved him, and out of Egypt I called my son." Like Moses, Jesus was rescued from a king so desperate to protect his reign that he murdered a generation of baby boys. But things are oddly flipped in this passage. While Israel is rescued from Pharaoh, the King of Egypt, Jesus is rescued from Herod, the King of the Jews! While the Hebrews were brought out of Egypt into Israel, Jesus was brought out of Israel into Egypt! This is how deeply we need a savior: even Israel, God's people, became corrupt like Egypt.

Where Moses was saved from Pharoah and placed in a basket, Jesus was saved from Herod and placed in a manger. While Israel was saved from their Egyptian slavemasters, Jesus came to save us from our greatest slavemasters: sin and death. And though Jesus was spared the violence of Herod, he accomplished our great Exodus by submitting to the violence of the cross. When he was torn on the cross, he tore down the darkness. Why? To free you and bring you into the most wonderful joy in him. To be united to Christ by faith is to know this deliverance!

Whatever your situation might be this season, don't despair. Lift up your hearts and remember that Christ was born into darkness to save us from it. He has not failed! This calls for feasting and celebration! Invite others into the joy! May the Lord give you hearts this season that rejoice in his deliverance!

Liturgy

LORD of our deliverance,

We praise you for waging war against the darkness
on our behalf!
Out of Egypt, you called your Son!

Your Son is our greater Moses, our King of Peace,
and our Great Deliverer!
He was born to save us from the darkness of sin
and the hand of tyrants.
In Christ, you parted the seas of death
and brought us into the promised land!

Let us remember and give thanks that our King was born
into enemy territory for the love of his enemies.

Week 4: Lord's Day Evening

Let us remember that he was saved in infancy from
Herod, so that later he would save sinners by not being
spared himself.
Let us remember and rejoice that in his body,
torn upon the cross,
Light has truly invaded the darkness of our world.

Give us hearts to celebrate with joy!
For sin, our slavemaster was cast into the sea!
Give us peace in Christ our Lord and Jesus our King!

Amen.

WEEK 4 — Midweek Evening

The Promised City of Christmas

Devotional and Liturgy by Pastor Ryan James

> *⁶ But as it is, they desire a better country, that is, a heavenly one. Therefore God is not ashamed to be called their God, for he has prepared for them a city.* — Hebrews 11:16 (ESV)

When I was younger, I romanticized the idea of celebrating Christmas in a big city. I can't put my finger on exactly what about it I found appealing, but I strongly suspect it had something to do with my love for the greatest Christmas movie of all time: Home Alone 2: Lost in New York. Watching Kevin McCallister roam around New York City, eat loads of junk food, and take out idiot bad guys was more formative than I'd care to admit.

Sadly, not only did I never get to booby trap an old brownstone apartment, but Christmas in the city has completely lost its allure for me. Seattle, specifically, has become a bit of a dumpster fire, and spending time there is now something I try to avoid.

As Christians, the unraveling of our society ought to concern us, but not in a way that leads to our cultural disengagement. Rather, Christmas ought to spur us on to see the disintegration of our cities as both a call toward Christian culture building and a reminder that a better city is coming.

When God created the world, he gave Adam a job. Adam's job was to fill the earth and subdue it, cultivating and taking dominion over God's creation for the sake of human flourishing.

This is still the task given to us, and Christmastime affords us a unique opportunity. You see, the more defiantly depraved our culture becomes, the more of a dissident you will be simply by continuing to celebrate Christmas in the ways you always have.

When you put up your tree, you are building a little Christian city, planting a flag for Christ's reign here on earth. Dads, when you lead your families in worship, singing Christmas carols joyfully with cups of hot cocoa in hand, you are confessing that Christ is Lord over all creation as far as the curse is found. Moms, when you bake your special Christmas cookies, you are filling your home with joy and the sweet aroma of the Gospel. As we disciple our children into the family of faith through our cherished traditions, we teach them what it means to be a people set apart from the world for God's pleasure and glory.

And the reason that these small celebrations of Christmas joy are powerful is because God himself works in exactly the same way.

God promised to send a King who would establish a better city. However, instead of showing up with full pomp and regalia to take command over Jerusalem, Jesus arrived quietly in the backwoods town of Bethlehem. While he was to usher in God's kingdom on earth, the city of his birth couldn't even be bothered to notice his arrival, let alone fall down before him in worship. And yet, Christ's humble incarnation was the exact means that God had planned to reclaim his covenant people and bring glory to his name.

This Christmas season, we look forward in hope to the promised city of God, New Jerusalem, where Christ will reign in glory over the whole earth. As we anticipate the celebration of his birth through our humble traditions and gatherings, may the light of Christ shine out brightly from our homes as beacons of hope, advance outposts of God's better city yet to come.

Week 4: Midweek Evening

Liturgy

Christ, in your birth, life, death, resurrection, and reign,
we find hope.
You entered our world in the humility of the manger.
Your first cries were heard by the lowly barn animals
present for your birth.
King of the Universe, you put on flesh
and came to dwell among us.

And in this world, you have given us a home.
You have called us to care for it, to cultivate it,
and to fill it with life.

Yet, like our father, Adam, we have failed.
Instead of setting our hands to the plow,
we have given them to idleness, wicked deeds, and deceit.
But God, though we have been content to sit lazily in the
wreckage of our sin, you are in the business of making
all things new.

Forgive us.

You saw our desolation, and you called us out of it.
Your wounds for our balm.
Your death for our life.
Your resurrection for ours.

And now you are preparing a new city for us,

The Promised City of Christmas

where all will be well and every wrong made right.
Help us to live even now as citizens of your kingdom,
New Jerusalem, where your glory will shine,
and kings will bring the glory of their nations
in submission to yours.
May we celebrate this Christmas in our homes
and families as little cities,
Outposts of Gospel peace, shining brightly
into the darkness around us.
That all might hear and believe that Christ is Lord.

Amen.

A Prayer for Christmas Morning

By Brynn James

> *¹⁵ When the angels went away from them into heaven, the shepherds said to one another, "Let us go over to Bethlehem and see this thing that has happened, which the Lord has made known to us." ¹⁶ And they went with haste and found Mary and Joseph, and the baby lying in a manger. ¹⁷ And when they saw it, they made known the saying that had been told them concerning this child. ¹⁸ And all who heard it wondered at what the shepherds told them. ¹⁹ But Mary treasured up all these things, pondering them in her heart. ²⁰ And the shepherds returned, glorifying and praising God for all they had heard and seen, as it had been told them.* — Luke 2:15-20 (ESV)

Heavenly Father, on this Christmas morn,
We give thanks for a gift undeserved:
An answer to our longing.

Christmas Day

A bright light in the darkness and hope of eternity.
Our long-awaited Savior, lowly yet magnificent.

Desire of all the nations: a tiny baby, the King
in whom our souls find their rest.
No crown upon thy sweet head, a manger for a throne,
in the royal company of peasants and livestock.
The first to look upon you with wonder were the rugged,
weathered, scruffy, disreputable, and anonymous.
While the elite were slumbering, the lowly were bowing.

An ordinary night no more.
An otherwise forgettable town is put on the map.
Shepherds become heralds,
A manger makes way for the mercy seat.

O God, that our Christmas celebration might be a
testament to your love of the ordinary.
Meager means, unlikely locations,
and we, your plain people.
For you did not come to reveal yourself to the perfect,
but to sinners.
Sinners whom you now send.
We are sent to proclaim, sent to build, sent to fight.
We commit to you our Christmas celebration that it may
be a proclamation, a diligent labor, and a battle.

As we look around at the twinkling lights, stockings
hung on the mantle, and cinnamon rolls baking in the

oven, help us to see these common pleasures as holy and transfigured. Each celebratory moment, a thrust of the sword in the fight against darkness and a declaration to our watching world. Like the shepherds, we do not simply hear the good news but we are renewed by it.

In this time of already-but-not-yet-ness, let us take heart that though the world may seem dark, you have already won. By thine all sufficient merit, there is hope:
Though the serpent sought to slay the child,
the Son was born to crush the snake himself.

Every Christmas, like a single brick laid in the wall of a cathedral, the mission of God advances. A multi-generational labor we may not live to see completed. Ordinary brick by ordinary brick, under the banner of the Lord, the joyful celebration of God's people will rattle the gates of hell itself.

God, give us eyes to see today the wonders you have made known to us. Like Mary, may we treasure them in our hearts, looking forward with an unshakable hope to the final end to our Advent longing. For we know you have not forgotten your people and will come again, raising us to your glorious throne.

Amen.

Christmas at Coram Deo Church

This Christmas, take some time out of your busy schedule to slow down and consider the message and meaning of Christmas. At Coram Deo Church, we will be offering multiple services to help us remember and savor the world-changing joy that only Christmas can bring us. We would love to have you join us.

CHRISTMAS EVE CANDLELIGHT SERVICES

Sunday, December 24 at **2, 3, 4,** & **5 p.m.**
Your RSVP is requested at coramdeochurch.org/christmas.

SUNDAY SERVICES

Weekly at **8, 9:30,** & **11 a.m.**
A class is available during our 9:30 and 11 a.m. services for kids who are 6 – 47 months old.

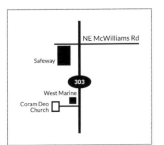

Directions available at
coramdeochurch.org/directions

5951 St Hwy 303 NE
Bremerton, WA 98311
360-377-0526 | coramdeochurch.org

Made in the USA
Columbia, SC
07 November 2023